The School Bus Song

W. T. Skye Garcia

The Alfred Signature Series

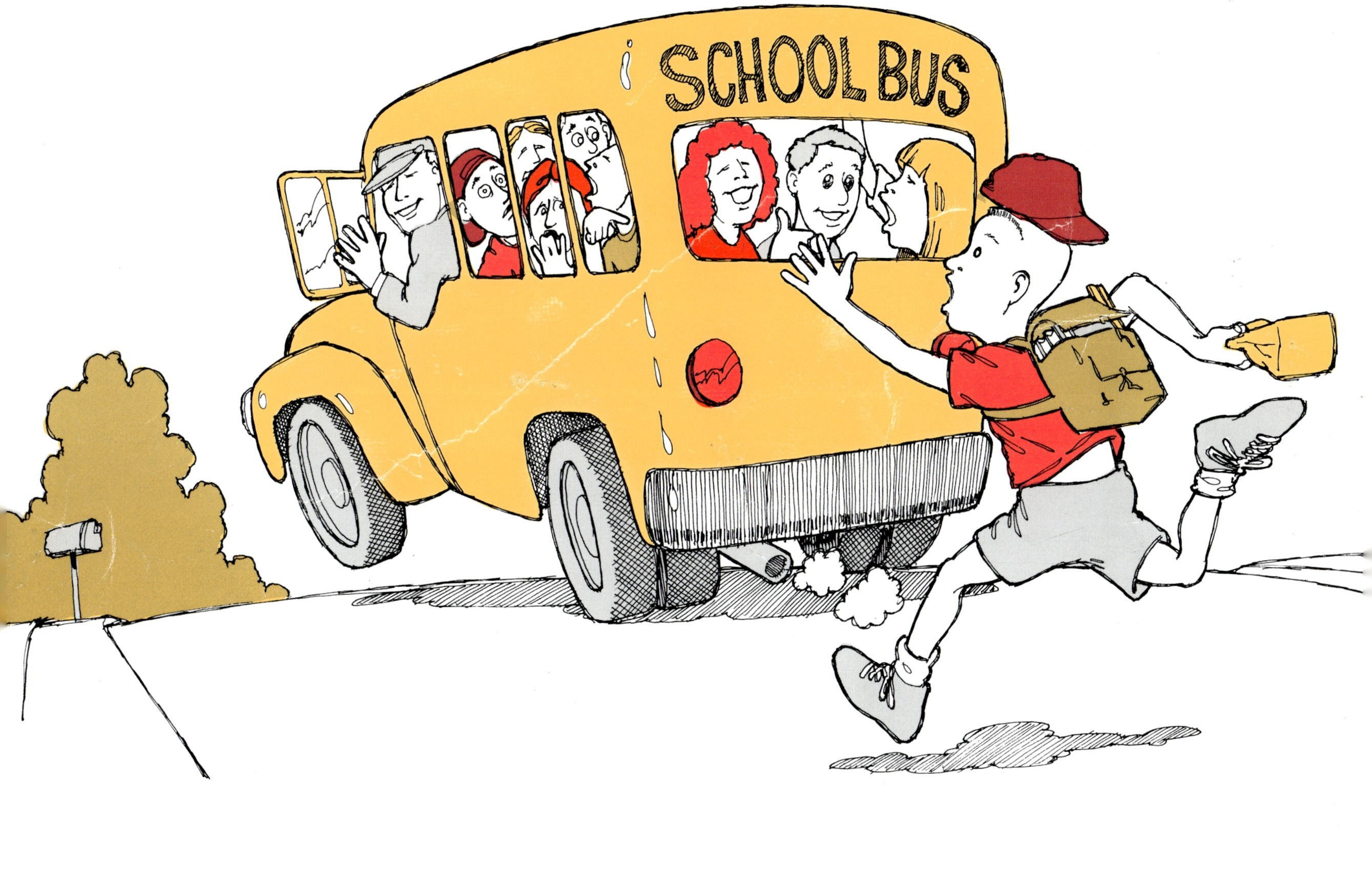

Designed to bring you the best in sheet music by today's most talented composers.

The School Bus Song

W. T. Skye Garcia

Movin' along

13
Eat a good break-fast, no time for play! Wash n' dress, comb my hair,

16
grab my gear. Got - ta run, school bus is here!
f
mp

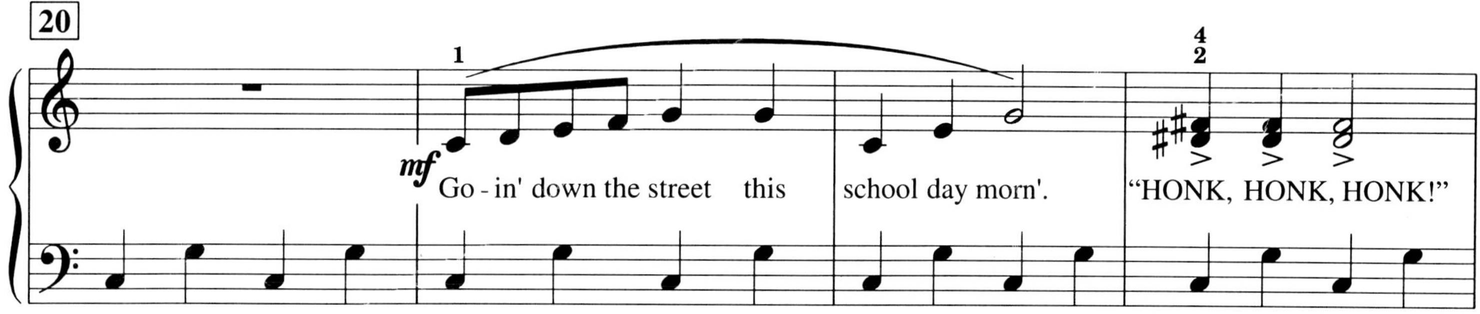
20
mf Go - in' down the street this school day morn'. "HONK, HONK, HONK!"

24
Sounds the horn. Pick-ing up the chil - dren where they wait.

27
RH 8va
As written
mp "HONK, HONK;
(fading away)
p HONK, HONK, HONK!" f School bus left me–I was late!
8va

The Alfred Signature Series
Sheet Music for Students of All Ages

Alfred is pleased to offer a wide variety of sheet music at many levels, from early elementary to early advanced. We select only the best music written by today's most talented composers. While some of our sheet music is directly correlated with Alfred's Basic Piano Library, most is loosely correlated so that teachers have flexibility in when and how to use this music effectively. The following guide shows the approximate correlations between the levels used in The Alfred Signature Series and Alfred's Basic Piano Library.

Early Elementary - Level 1A

Elementary - Level 1B

Late Elementary - Level 2

Early Intermediate - Level 3

Intermediate - Levels 4 and 5

Late Intermediate - Levels 5 and 6

Early Advanced - Level 6 +

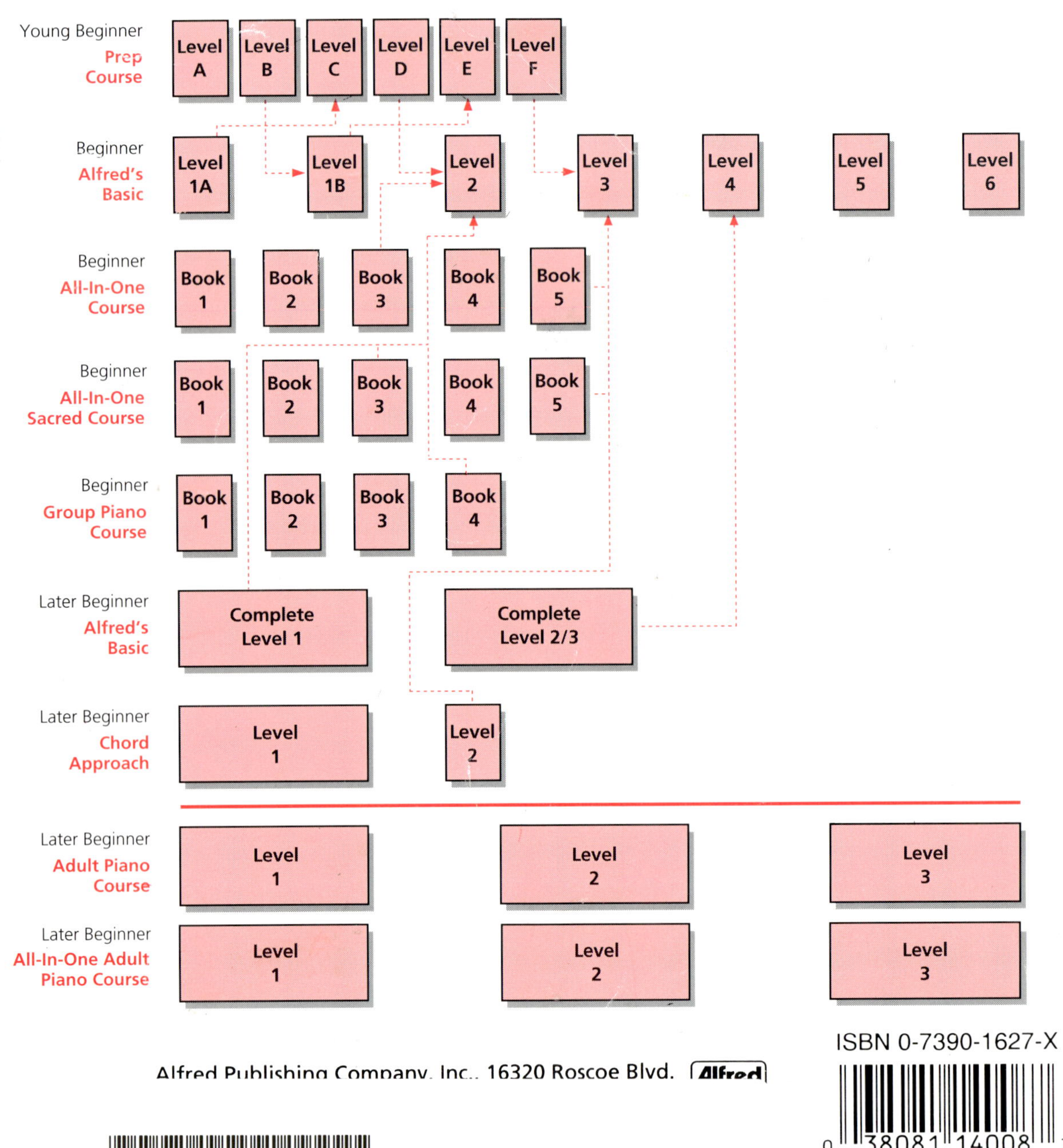

ISBN 0-7390-1627-X

Alfred Publishing Company, Inc. 16320 Roscoe Blvd. **Alfred**